SCHOLASTIC

BEST PRACTICES *in Action*

GRADES 3–4

Math Test Prep That Matters!

100 Standards-Based Math Prompts That Develop Students' Critical Thinking and Deepen Their Understanding of Key Math Concepts

JOSEPH A. PORZIO

NEW YORK • TORONTO • LONDON • AUCKLAND • SYDNEY
MEXICO CITY • NEW DELHI • HONG KONG • BUENOS AIRES

Teaching *Resources*

Cover design by Jason Robinson
Interior design by Holly Grundon
Interior illustrations by Teresa Anderko

ISBN-13: 978-0-439-59722-7
ISBN-10: 0-439-59722-6
Copyright © 2006 by Joseph A. Porzio
All rights reserved.
Printed in the USA.

1 2 3 4 5 6 7 8 9 10   31   15 14 13 12 11 10 09 08 07 06

Contents

Introduction

*In an age now driven by the relentless necessity
of scientific and technological advance, the current
preparation that students in the United States receive
in mathematics and science is, in a word, unacceptable.*

— Thomas L. Friedman, *The World Is Flat:
A Brief History of the Twenty-First Century*

Over the past three decades educators, business leaders, and policymakers calling for education reform have voiced deep concerns over our students' mathematics and science achievement (Clements, Sarama, & DiBiase, 2004). These concerns seem especially justified when we compare our students' scores on international tests, such as Trends in International Mathematics and Science Study (TIMSS), with those of students from other nations. In 2003, U.S. fourth-grade students ranked 12th out of 25 countries in math scores (International Association for the Evaluation of Educational Achievement, TIMSS, 2003).

In 1983, the U.S. Department of Education published the report "A Nation at Risk," often cited as the origin of current reform efforts. GOALS 2000, signed into law on March 31, 1994, listed a series of ambitious goals, which includes making the United States "first in the world in mathematics and science education." Even the National Assessment of Educational Progress (NAEP), the "Nation's Report Card," prompts repeated calls for reform. Just after the start of the new millennium, the federal government, through the No Child Left Behind Act (NCLB), expanded its role in education by establishing accountability and certification requirements that affected students, educators, and public schools across America. In his January 2006 State of the Union address, President George W. Bush announced ". . . an American Competitiveness Initiative to give our nation's children a firm grounding in math and science."

Clearly, there is more attention and recognition of the importance of mathematics (Kilpatrick, Swafford, & Findell, 2001) in a global economy where the vast majority of jobs require more sophisticated skills than jobs in the past required.

How can we—as regional/district leaders, site supervisors of mathematics, math coaches, classroom teachers, support staff in after-school academic intervention services, and parents—respond to the recognized needs in a manner that will lead to greater academic achievement in mathematics for all students?

Scholastic's Best Practices in Action series provides a definitive response to the call for action from those concerned with promoting and supporting challenging and rigorous classroom instructional practices, rooted in scientifically and/or evidence-based research. The series features promising best practices that impact teaching and learning by ensuring alignment between standards, assessment, and instruction. Among its key features is the recognition that clear, well-defined standards (what students are expected to know and be able to do at their grade level) have a positive impact on classroom teachers' instruction and students' learning.

The Mathematical Sciences Education Board's report "Everybody Counts" (1989) states: "We must ensure that tests measure what is of value, not just what is easy to test. If we want students to investigate, explore, and discover, assessment must not measure just mimicry mathematics." Further, the six key principles in the National Council of Teachers of Mathematics (NCTM) *Principles and Standards for School Mathematics* describe specific features of high-quality mathematics education. Educators who know the value of integrating content and process standards are eager to find supportive resources that complement their mathematics program.

Math Test Prep That Matters! fulfills this need and features a collection of challenging activities designed to promote thinking and foster communication through development of mathematical language (process standards) while enhancing mathematical concepts and their related skills (content standards). This book was written in direct response to the increased attention in mathematics, including that in the formative early childhood years where early childhood educators—the foundation builders—are developing students' understanding of mathematical concepts and their related skills. The challenges found in *Math Test Prep That Matters!* provide opportunities for investigations and rigorous activities that are based in content and designed to promote thinking and oral and written communication skills.

What Does It Mean to Be Proficient in Mathematics?

While we have witnessed profound swings during the past years in what it means to be successful in mathematics (e.g., new math, back to basics, NCTM's Agenda for Action which focused on problem solving), we now recognize that math proficiency requires much more than facility in using computational procedures in arithmetic.

In November 2004, the New York State Education Department's Mathematics Standards Committee presented its recommendations to the New York State Board of Regents, based upon numerous references, including *Principles and Standards for School Mathematics* (NCTM, 2000), *Adding It Up: Helping Children Learn Mathematics* (National Research Council, 2001), *Engaging Young Children in Mathematics: Standards for Early Childhood Mathematics Education* (Lawrence Erlbaum Associates, 2004), and *The Math We Need to "Know" and "Do"* (Corwin Press, 2000). The committee recognized that "every teacher of mathematics, whether at the elementary, middle, or high school level, has an individual goal to provide students with the knowledge and understanding of the mathematics necessary to function in a world that is very dependent upon the application of mathematics. Instructionally, this goal translates into three components:

1. Conceptual understanding
2. Procedural fluency
3. Problem solving"

These components are integrally related and need to be taught simultaneously and should be a component of every lesson.

From Research to Practice

How does *Math Test Prep That Matters!* support, complement, and improve student achievement in mathematics in the classroom?

- It promotes the use of promising instructional practices that are rooted in scientifically/evidence-based research, as defined in the U.S. Department of Education's website at www.ed.gov and its link to the What Works Clearinghouse. (NOTE: On May 15th, 2006, U.S. Secretary of Education Margaret Spellings announced the names of seventeen expert panelists to comprise the National Mathematics Advisory Panel. The panel's findings and determinations in the area of mathematics will serve as a basis for building capacity and proficiency in the area of mathematics.)

- It develops conceptual understanding and their related skills while promoting communication, reasoning, and thinking. Focusing instruction on the meaningful development of important mathematical ideas increases the level of student understanding (Brownell, 1945). There is a long history of research on the effects of teaching for meaning and understanding.

- It provides several opportunities through the graphic prompts for students to invent new knowledge through non-routine problems. Teachers should periodically introduce a lesson involving a new skill by posing it as a problem to be solved and regularly allow students to build new knowledge based on their intuitive knowledge and informal procedures. Students learn both concepts and skills by solving problems (Cobb, 1991).

- It stimulates whole-class discussion following individual and group work. In addition to promoting communication, this serves as an effective diagnostic tool. Research suggests that teachers should provide opportunities such as activities, problems, and assignments for students to interact (i.e., work in small groups and share ideas) in problem-rich situations (Davidson, 1985).

More Research to Support the Use of <u>Math Test Prep That Matters!</u>

- Teaching math with a focus on number sense encourages students to become problem solvers in a wide variety of situations and to view mathematics as a discipline that is important (Markovits & Sowder, 1994; Cobb, 1991).

- Long-term use of concrete materials is positively related to increases in student mathematics achievement and improved attitudes towards mathematics (Suydam & Higgins, 1977; Driscoll, 1990). In a recent meta-analysis of sixty studies (kindergarten through post-secondary) that compared the effects of using concrete materials with the effects of more abstract instruction, Sowell (1989) found that long-term use of concrete materials by teachers knowledgeable in their use improved student achievement and attitudes. John van de Walle's translation model demonstrates how we can develop understanding from one external representation of an idea to another (van de Walle, 1998; Lesh, Post, & Behr, 1987).

- Numerous studies of mathematics achievement at different grade and ability levels show that students benefit when real objects (manipulatives) are used as aids in learning mathematics (Bennett, 1986).

- *EDThoughts: What We Know About Mathematics Teaching and Learning* offers numerous citings related to effective instructional methods where time is allotted for students to individually ponder appropriate strategies; identify necessary tools to assist in solving the problem; work in small groups exploring and discussing ideas and solving the problem; and report their findings to the class (Sutton, 2002).

How to Use This Book

The standards-based prompts in this book are arranged by the content and process strands typically found in an NCTM standards-based curriculum. The prompts feature graphics similar to those in student texts and on formative and normative assessments, further supporting the alignment of standards, assessment, and instruction. Offer these graphic prompts only after you have instructed students on the basic concepts using practices that include hands-on/concrete manipulatives, models, and representations (Sowell, 1989).

The graphic prompts are designed so that students can easily recognize the content area highlighted and then develop a written and/or oral response to the graphic. This strategy helps build students' content knowledge (conceptual understanding and their related skills) while developing and strengthening their process skills (i.e., problem solving, reasoning and proof, oral and written communication, connections, and representation). The graphic prompts across all content and process strands are designed to promote thinking, reasoning, problem solving, and oral and written communication (Sutton, 2002).

After students have shared their responses to a graphic prompt, you may wish to offer a challenge or extension related to the same prompt. Embedded assessment helps you determine a student's level of understanding of content based upon his or her responses. Following are some examples of how you can use the graphic prompts to assess students' learning and further challenge them:

Number and Operations

Page 15: If necessary, guide students to recognize that the units are metric (meters). A typical student question might be: *What are the numbers in order from least to greatest or from greatest to least?* Challenge students to convert the units shown to centimeters (cm).

Algebra

Page 32: Guide students to discover how squares are found within the models. For example, the 2 x 2 grid shows four squares but has one additional surrounding square (for a total of five squares). Students might ask: *How many squares would there be in a 5 x 5 grid?* As an extension, challenge students to find out how many squares are on a checkerboard. HINT: Begin in the lower left-hand corner and think:

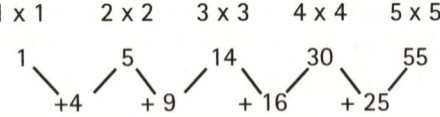

Geometry

Page 37: Encourage students to create a rectangular model similar to the graphic on the page and measure its length and width to find its area. Have them cut out a triangle from one end (as shown in the graphic) and move it to the other end of the model. Students might ask: *What has changed? (The shape/figure is now a parallelogram.) What has not changed? (The area remains the same.)* The area of a parallelogram is A = bh. Challenge students to explore and investigate how the formula for a triangle can be derived from this model. (HINT: Draw a diagonal to see that A = 1/2 bh). (The model on page 38 shows the area of a triangle (A = 1/2 bh) is half of the rectangle (A = lw).

Measurement

Page 45: Students analyze the data in the hand-span chart and notice the difference between estimated and actual measurements. Students might ask: *Who made the best estimate? Who had the widest hand span?* As an extension, have students estimate the height of students in centimeters and then measure to find the actual heights. Later, in a separate column, have them convert the centimeters to meters, e.g., 162 cm = 1.62 m.

Data Analysis and Probability

Page 49: Students might ask: *What kind of graph would best show the number of cans collected?* Guide students to create an appropriate graph. Challenge them to include all components of a graph: title, labels, calibration (scale), start at zero, bar graph with bars that have the same width, vertical/horizontal bars.

Problem Solving

Page 54: A typical question students might ask would be: *How many handshakes were there?* Guide students to use a problem-solving strategy to investigate the handshake problem. They may consider acting out the problem, drawing a picture, making a simpler problem, or creating a chart/table. Challenge students to discover a pattern and possibly derive a formula.

Reasoning and Proof

Page 57: Students should notice that all squares are cut in half, including D. Some students might ask: *How do you know that all squares are cut in half?* Challenge students to create two unusual halves and have them explain their solution by proving they have two halves (e.g., showing congruence).

Communication

Page 59: Some students may recognize the tangram puzzle pieces and ask: *What combination of pieces weigh half a pound?* Encourage students to create a square using the seven tangram pieces. Assign a value or weight to the whole tangram (e.g., 48 grams) and challenge students to find the value or weight of each piece. Challenge students to find three pieces that have the same area and to explain how they know the areas are the same.

Connections

Page 61: Guide students to make connections between mathematics and other subject areas, such as social studies. A typical student question might be: *What is the distance between Washington, D.C., and Los Angeles?* Ask students to explain components of different maps, e.g., scale, key, legend, colors, boundary lines. Challenge them to find the distance between two other major cities in the United States.

Representation

Page 62: Create a variety of models that depict multiplication of fractions. Guide students to understand how the model is related to the algorithm. Challenge students to study the model and the algorithm and create an accompanying problem.

Bibliography

Resources for Developing, Supporting, and Strengthening Mathematical Proficiency

Bennett, W. J. (1986). *What works: Research about teaching and learning.* Washington, DC: United States Department of Education.

Broad Prize for Urban Education. (2002). *Showcasing success/Rewarding achievement.* Austin, TX: National Center for Educational Accountability.

Brownell, W. A. (1945). When is arithmetic meaningful? *Journal of Education Research, 38,* 481–498.

Clements, D. H., Sarama, J., & DiBiase, A.-M. (Eds.). (2004). *Engaging young children in mathematics: Standards for early childhood mathematics education.* Mahwah, NJ: Erlbaum.

Cobb, P. et al. (1991). Assessment of a problem-centered second-grade mathematics project. *Journal for Research in Mathematics Education, 22,* 3–29.

Davidson, N. (1985). Small-group cooperative learning in mathematics: A selective view of the research. In R. Hertz-Lazarowitz, S. Kagan, S. Sharan, R. Slavin, & C. Webb (Eds.), *Learning to Cooperate, Cooperating to Learn* (pp. 211–230). New York: Plenum.

Driscoll, M. J. (1982). *Research within reach: Elementary school mathematics.* Reston, VA: National Council of Teachers of Mathematics.

Driscoll, M. J. (1990). The teacher's role: Manipulatives from The bridge from concrete to abstract. In M. J. Driscoll, *Research within reach: Elementary school mathematics* (6th printing). Reston, VA: National Council of Teachers of Mathematics.

Friedman, T. L. (2005). *The world is flat: A brief history of the twenty-first century.* New York: Farrar, Straus & Giroux.

GOALS 2000: Educate America Act. (1994, March 31). Pub. Law 103-227 (108 Stat.125)

Kilpatrick, J., Swafford, J., & Findell, B. (Eds.). (2001). *Adding it up: Helping children learn mathematics.* Washington, DC: National Academy Press.

Lesh, R. A., Post, T. R., & Behr, M. J. (1987). Representations and translations among representations in mathematics learning and problem solving." In C. Janvier (Ed.), *Problems of representation in the teaching and learning of mathematics* (pp. 33–40). Hillsdale, NJ: Erlbaum.

Markovits, Z., & Sowder, J. (1994). Developing number sense: An intervention study in grade 7. *Journal for Research in Mathematics Education, 25,* 4–29.

National Research Council. (1989). *Everybody counts: A report to the nation on the future of mathematics education.* Washington, DC: National Academies Press

National Assessment of Educational Progress (NAEP). National Center for Educational Statistics. Institute of Educational Sciences. United States Department of Education. http://nces.ed.gov/nationsreportcard/

National Commission of Excellence in Education. (1983). *A nation at risk: The imperative for educational reform.* Washington, DC: U.S. Government Printing Office.

New York State Education Department. (2005, March). *Mathematics core curriculum.* http://www.emsc.nysed.gov /ciai/mst/mathstandards/revised3.htm

Principles and standards for school mathematics. (2000). Reston, VA: National Council of Teachers of Mathematics.

Solomon, P. G. (2000). *The math we need to "know" and "do": Content standards for elementary and middle grades.* Thousand Oaks, CA: Corwin Press.

Sowell, E. J. (1989). Effects of manipulative materials in mathematics instruction. *Journal for Research in Mathematics Education, 20,* 409–505.

Stenmark, J. K. (Ed.). (1991). *Mathematics assessment: Myths, models, good questions and practical suggestions.* Reston, VA: National Council of Teachers of Mathematics.

Sutton, J., & Krueger, A. (Eds.). (2002). *EDThoughts: What we know about mathematics teaching and learning.* Aurora: CO: Mid-Continental Research for Education and Learning.

Suydam, M. N., & Higgins, J. L. (1977). *Activity-based learning in elementary school mathematics: Recommendations from research.* Columbus, OH: ERIC/Clearinghouse for Science, Mathematics, and Environmental Education.

Trends in International Mathematics and Science Study. International Association for the Evaluation of Educational Achievement. U.S. Department of Education. http://nces.ed.gov/timss/

Van de Walle, J. A. (1998). *Elementary and middle school mathematics: Teaching developmentally* (3rd ed.). New York: Addison Wesley Longman.

NCTM Standards

Standard – Instructional programs from Pre-kindergarten through Grade 12 should enable all students to:	Expectations – In Grades 3-5, all students should:

I: Number and Operations

A. Understand numbers, ways of representing numbers, relationships among numbers, and number systems

1. Understand the place-value structure of the base-ten number system and be able to represent and compare whole numbers and decimals;
2. Recognize equivalent representations for the same number and generate them by decomposing and composing numbers;
3. Develop understanding of fractions as parts of unit wholes, as parts of a collection, as locations on number lines, and as divisions of whole numbers;
4. Use models, benchmarks, and equivalent forms to judge the size of fractions;
5. Recognize and generate equivalent forms of commonly used fractions, decimals, and percents;
6. Explore numbers less than 0 by extending the number line and through familiar applications;
7. Describe classes of numbers according to characteristics such as the nature of their factors.

B. Understand meanings of operations and how they relate to one another

1. Understand various meanings of multiplication and division;
2. Understand the effects of multiplying and dividing whole numbers;
3. Identify and use relationships between operations, such as division as the inverse of multiplication, to solve problems;
4. Understand and use properties of operations, such as the distributivity of multiplication over addition.

C. Compute fluently and make reasonable estimates

1. Develop fluency with basic number combinations for multiplication and division and use these combinations to mentally compute related problems, such as 30 x 50;
2. Develop fluency in adding, subtracting, multiplying, and dividing whole numbers;
3. Develop and use strategies to estimate the results of whole-number computations and to judge the reasonableness of such results;
4. Develop and use strategies to estimate computations involving fractions and decimals in situations relevant to students' experience;
5. Use visual models, benchmarks, and equivalent forms to add and subtract commonly used fractions and decimals;
6. Select appropriate methods and tools for computing with whole numbers from among mental computation, estimation, calculators, and paper and pencil according to the context and nature of the computation and use the selected method or tool.

II. Algebra

A. Understand patterns, relations, and functions

1. Describe, extend, and make generalizations about geometric and numeric patterns;
2. Represent and analyze patterns and functions, using words, tables, and graphs.

B. Represent and analyze mathematical situations and structures using algebraic symbols

1. Identify such properties as commutativity, associativity, and distributivity and use them to compute with whole numbers;
2. Represent the idea of a variable as an unknown quantity using a letter or a symbol;
3. Express mathematical relationships using equations.

C. Use mathematical models to represent and understand quantitative relationships

1. Model problem situations with objects and use representations such as graphs, tables, and equations to draw conclusions.

D. Analyze change in various contexts

1. Investigate how a change in one variable relates to a change in a second variable;
2. Identify and describe situations with constant or varying rates of change and compare them.

III. Geometry

A. Analyze characteristics and properties of two- and three-dimensional geometric shapes and develop mathematical arguments about geometric relationships

1. Identify, compare, and analyze attributes of two- and three-dimensional shapes and develop vocabulary to describe the attributes;
2. Classify two- and three-dimensional shapes according to their properties and develop definitions of classes of shapes such as triangles and pyramids;
3. Investigate, describe, and reason about the results of subdividing, combining, and transforming shapes;
4. Explore congruence and similarity;
5. Make and test conjectures about geometric properties and relationships and develop logical arguments to justify conclusions.

Standard – Instructional programs from Pre-kindergarten through Grade 12 should enable all students to:	Expectations – In Grades 3-5, all students should:	
B. Specify locations and describe spatial relationships using coordinate geometry and other representational systems	1. Describe location and movement using common language and geometric vocabulary; 2. Make and use coordinate systems to specify locations and to describe paths; 3. Find the distance between points along horizontal and vertical lines of a coordinate system.	III. Geometry
C. Apply transformations and use symmetry to analyze mathematical situations	1. Predict and describe the results of sliding, flipping, and turning two-dimensional shapes; 2. Describe a motion or a series of motions that will show that two shapes are congruent; 3. Identify and describe line and rotational symmetry in two- and three-dimensional shapes and designs.	
D. Use visualization, spatial reasoning, and geometric modeling to solve problems	1. Build and draw geometric objects; 2. Create and describe mental images of objects, patterns, and paths; 3. Identify and build a three-dimensional object from two-dimensional representations of that object; 4. Identify and draw a two-dimensional representation of a three-dimensional object; 5. Use geometric models to solve problems in other areas of mathematics, such as number and measurement; 6. Recognize geometric ideas and relationships and apply them to other disciplines and to problems that arise in the classroom or in everyday life.	
A. Understand measurable attributes of objects and the units, systems, and processes of measurement	1. Understand such attributes as length, area, weight, volume, and size of angle and select the appropriate type of unit for measuring each attribute; 2. Understand the need for measuring with standard units and become familiar with standard units in the customary and metric systems; 3. Carry out simple unit conversions, such as from centimeters to meters, within a system of measurement; 4. Understand that measurements are approximations and understand how differences in units affect precision; 5. Explore what happens to measurements of a two-dimensional shape such as its perimeter and area when the shape is changed in some way.	IV. Measurement
B. Apply appropriate techniques, tools, and formulas to determine measurements	1. Develop strategies for estimating the perimeters, areas, and volumes of irregular shapes; 2. Select and apply appropriate standard units and tools to measure length, area, volume, weight, time, temperature, and the size of angles; 3. Select and use benchmarks to estimate measurements; 4. Develop, understand, and use formulas to find the area of rectangles and related triangles and parallelograms; 5. Develop strategies to determine the surface areas and volumes of rectangular sides.	
A. Formulate questions that can be addressed with data and collect, organize, and display relevant data to answer them	1. Design investigations to address a question and consider how data-collection methods affect the nature of the data set; 2. Collect data using observations, surveys, and experiments; 3. Represent data using tables and graphs such as line plots, bar graphs, and line graphs; 4. Recognize the differences in representing categorical and numerical data.	V. Data Analysis and Probability
B. Select and use appropriate statistical methods to analyze data	1. Describe the shape and important features of a set of data and compare related data sets, with an emphasis on how the data are distributed; 2. Use measures of center, focusing on the median, and understand what each does and does not indicate about the data set; 3. Compare different representations of the same data and evaluate how well each representation shows important aspects of the data.	
C. Develop and evaluate inferences and predictions that are based on data	1. Propose and justify conclusions and predictions that are based on data and design studies to further investigate the conclusions or predictions.	
D. Understand and apply basic concepts of probability	1. Describe events as likely or unlikely and discuss the degree of likelihood using such words as *certain*, *equally likely*, and *impossible*; 2. Predict the probability of outcomes of simple experiments and test the predictions; 3. Understand that the measure of the likelihood of an event can be represented by a number from 0 to 1.	

	Standard – Instructional programs from Pre-kindergarten through Grade 12 should enable all students to:
VI. Problem Solving	**A.** Build new mathematical knowledge through problem solving;
	B. Solve problems that arise in mathematics and in other contexts;
	C. Apply and adapt a variety of appropriate strategies to solve problems;
	D. Monitor and reflect on the process of mathematical problem solving.
VII. Reasoning and Proof	**A.** Recognize reasoning and proof as fundamental aspects of mathematics;
	B. Make and investigate mathematical conjectures;
	C. Develop and evaluate mathematical arguments and proofs;
	D. Select and use various types of reasoning and methods of proof.
VIII. Communication	**A.** Organize and consolidate their mathematical thinking through communication;
	B. Communicate their mathematical thinking coherently and clearly to peers, teachers, and others;
	C. Analyze and evaluate the mathematical thinking and strategies of others;
	D. Use the language of mathematics to express mathematical ideas precisely.
IX. Connections	**A.** Recognize and use connections among mathematical ideas;
	B. Understand how mathematical ideas interconnect and build on one another to produce a coherent whole;
	C. Recognize and apply mathematics in contexts outside of mathematics.
X. Representation	**A.** Create and use representations to organize, record, and communicate mathematical ideas;
	B. Select, apply, and translate among mathematical representations to solve problems;
	C. Use representations to model and interpret physical, social, and mathematical phenomena.

* Standards notation on activity pages:
  S: I A / E: 1 means the activity meets the Number & Operations (I)
  Standard A (Understand numbers, ways of representing numbers, . . .),
  Expectation 1 (Understand the place-value structure . . .).

Name: _____ Date: _____

**Six million thirty-five thousand
five hundred eighteen**

1. Write about what you see above.
   _____
   _____

2. Ask a question about it.
   _____
   _____

3. Answer your question.
   _____
   _____

S: I A / E: 1

Name: _____ Date: _____

$$
\begin{array}{r}
5 \\
70 \\
800 \\
4{,}000 \\
\boxed{} \\
900{,}000 \\
+\ 6{,}000{,}000 \\
\hline
6{,}0\,\bigcirc\,24{,}\square\,75
\end{array}
$$

1. Write about what you see above.
   _____
   _____

2. Ask a question about it.
   _____
   _____

3. Answer your question.
   _____
   _____

S: I A / E: 1

Name: _____   Date: _____

A. 924 (>) 429

B. 5,238 (<) 8,325

C. 7,512 ( ) 7,251

D. 8,429 ( ) 8,924

1. Write about what you see above.

_____

_____

2. Ask a question about it.

_____

_____

3. Answer your question.

_____

_____

S: I A / E: 1

Name: _____   Date: _____

three hundred six

306

two hundred forty-five

[ ]

1. Write about what you see above.

_____

_____

2. Ask a question about it.

_____

_____

3. Answer your question.

_____

_____

S: I A / E: 1

Name: _____   Date: _____

A	B
0.7 m	0.09 m
C	D
0.25 m	0.85 m

1. Write about what you see above.

_____

2. Ask a question about it.

_____

3. Answer your question.

_____

S I A / E: 1

Name: _____   Date: _____

$ .52   ◯ $ .25

$ .09   ◯ $ .78

1. Write about what you see above.

_____

2. Ask a question about it.

_____

3. Answer your question.

_____

S: I A / E: 1

Number and Operations

Name: _____ Date: _____

A	B
40 + 8 = ⬜	4 dozen

C	D
8 x 6 = ⬜	IIL

1. Write about what you see above.

_____

_____

2. Ask a question about it.

_____

_____

3. Answer your question.

_____

_____

S: I A / E: 2

Number and Operations

Name: _____ Date: _____

A

B

0.5

⬜

1. Write about what you see above.

_____

_____

2. Ask a question about it.

_____

_____

3. Answer your question.

_____

_____

S: I A / E: 1

Name: _____ Date: _____

48 Pencils

1. Write about what you see above.

_____

2. Ask a question about it.

_____

3. Answer your question.

_____

S: I A / E: 3

Name: _____ Date: _____

Make one dollar with these coins.

A   B

ONE DOLLAR

C   D

1. Write about what you see above.

_____

2. Ask a question about it.

_____

3. Answer your question.

_____

S: I A / E: 2

Name: _____ Date: _____

$$8, \boxed{} , 56$$

$8 \times \boxed{} = 56$	$56 \div \boxed{} = 8$
$\boxed{} \times 8 = 56$	$56 \div 8 = \boxed{}$

1. Write about what you see above.

_____

2. Ask a question about it.

_____

3. Answer your question.

_____

S: I A / E: 2

Name: _____ Date: _____

A	B
$2 \times 2 \times 2 \times 2$	$4 \times \bigcirc$
C	D
$8 + \triangle$	$\boxed{}$ ounces in one pound

16

1. Write about what you see above.

_____

2. Ask a question about it.

_____

3. Answer your question.

_____

S: I A / E: 2

Name: _____ Date: _____

**one
whole**

1. **Write about what you see above.**

_____

_____

2. **Ask a question about it.**

_____

_____

3. **Answer your question.**

_____

_____

Name: _____ Date: _____

one whole						
one half			one half			
one fourth		one fourth		one fourth		one fourth
one eighth	one eighth	one eighth	one eighth	one eighth	one eighth	one eighth	one eighth

1. **Write about what you see above.**

_____

_____

2. **Ask a question about it.**

_____

_____

3. **Answer your question.**

_____

_____

Name: _____ Date: _____

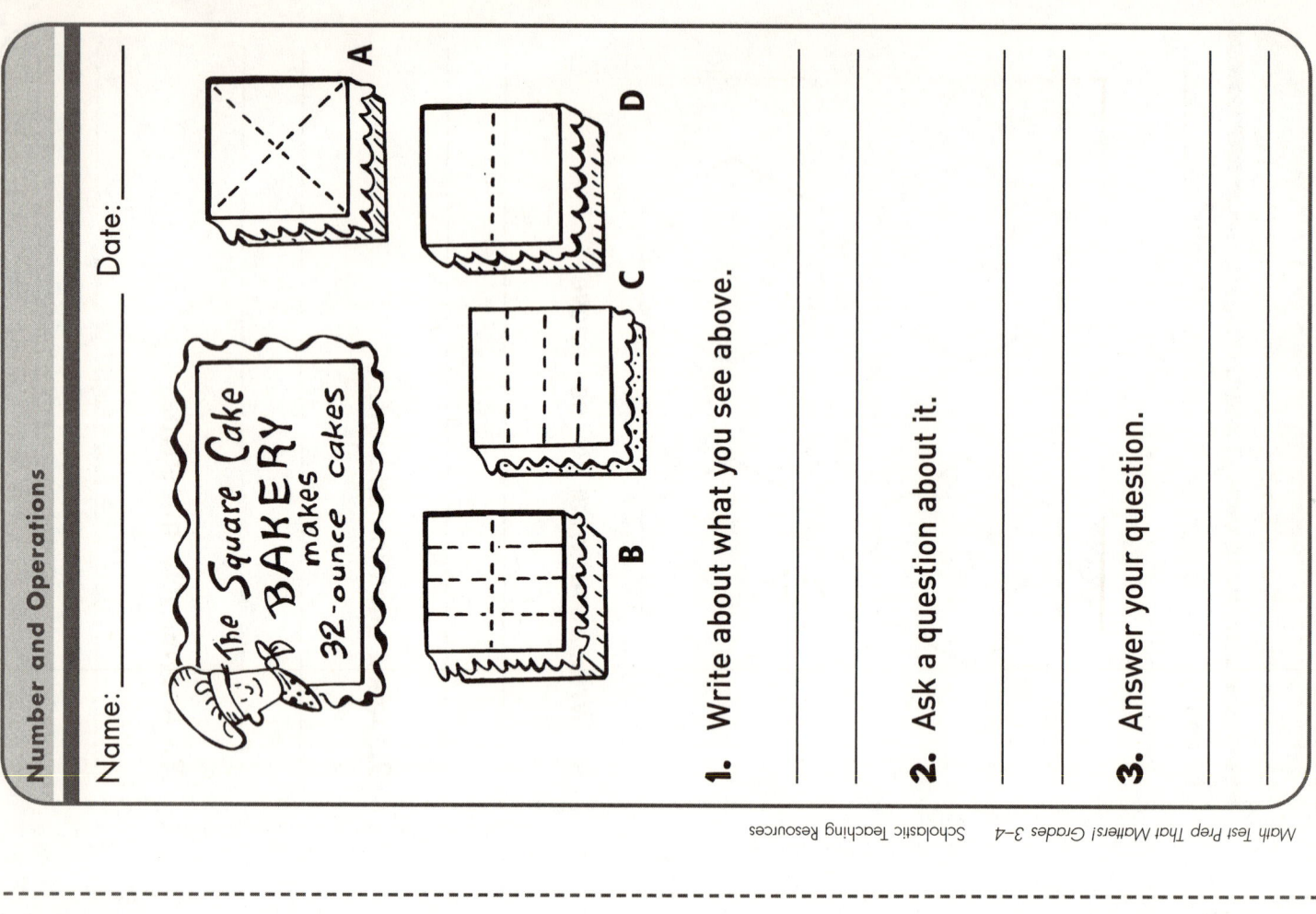

The Square Cake BAKERY makes 32-ounce cakes

A B C D

1. Write about what you see above.

_____
_____

2. Ask a question about it.

_____
_____

3. Answer your question.

_____
_____

S: I A / E: 4

Name: _____ Date: _____

0    $\frac{1}{5}$ A   1

0   0.2   0.5   B   1.0

0   C $.50 $1.00

1. Write about what you see above.

_____
_____

2. Ask a question about it.

_____
_____

3. Answer your question.

_____
_____

S: I A / E: 3, 4

Name: _____   Date: _____

A	B
	0.8
C	D
$\dfrac{4}{5}$	**20%**

1. Write about what you see above.

_____

_____

2. Ask a question about it.

_____

_____

3. Answer your question.

_____

_____

S: I A / E: 5

Name: _____   Date: _____

A	B
	0.75
C	D
$\dfrac{3}{4}$	**75%**

1. Write about what you see above.

_____

_____

2. Ask a question about it.

_____

_____

3. Answer your question.

_____

_____

S: I A / E: 5

Number and Operations

Name: _____   Date: _____

The temperature at 11:00 P.M. was 10 degrees colder.

1. Write about what you see above.

_____

_____

2. Ask a question about it.

_____

_____

3. Answer your question.

_____

_____

S: I A / E: 6

Number and Operations

Name: _____   Date: _____

1. Write about what you see above.

_____

_____

2. Ask a question about it.

_____

_____

3. Answer your question.

_____

_____

S: I A / E: 6

Name: _____ Date: _____

-6 -5 -4 -3 -2 -1 0 1 2 3 4 5 6

+4

-6

$$4 + (-6) = \boxed{}$$

1. Write about what you see above.

_____

2. Ask a question about it.

_____

3. Answer your question.

_____

S: I A / E: 6

Name: _____ Date: _____

-6 -5 -4 -3 -2 -1 0 1 2 3 4 5 6

Symbol	■	★	●
Number	-6	3	-5
Opposite	+6	-3	

1. Write about what you see above.

_____

2. Ask a question about it.

_____

3. Answer your question.

_____

S: I A / E: 6

Name: _____   Date: _____

Number	Factors	Number of Factors
1	1	1
2	1, 2	2
3	1, 3	2
4	1, 2, 4	3
5	1, 5	2
	1, 2, 3, 6	4
7		2
8	1, 2, 4, 8	
12		

1. Write about what you see above.

_____

2. Ask a question about it.

_____

3. Answer your question.

_____

Name: _____   Date: _____

1. Write about what you see above.

_____

2. Ask a question about it.

_____

3. Answer your question.

_____

Number and Operations

Name: _____   Date: _____

Group 1

A
B
C

Group 2

A
B
C

1. Write about what you see above.

_____

2. Ask a question about it.

_____

3. Answer your question.

_____

S: I A / E: 7

Number and Operations

Name: _____   Date: _____

5, 7, 35	
5 x [ ] = 35	35 ÷ [ ] = 5
[ ] x 5 = 35	35 ÷ 5 = [ ]

6, [ ], 48	

1. Write about what you see above.

_____

2. Ask a question about it.

_____

3. Answer your question.

_____

S: I B / E: 1

Number and Operations

Name: _____ Date: _____

23 Passengers

Grade 4
trip to
museum:
192 Students

1. Write about what you see above.

_____

_____

2. Ask a question about it.

_____

3. Answer your question.

_____

_____

S: I B / E: 2

Number and Operations

Name: _____ Date: _____

1. Write about what you see above.

_____

_____

2. Ask a question about it.

_____

3. Answer your question.

_____

_____

S: I B / E: 2

Name: _____ Date: _____

Distributive Property

36 x 12 =

36 x (10 + ☐) =

(36 x 10) + (36 x ☐)

1. Write about what you see above.

_____

_____

2. Ask a question about it.

_____

3. Answer your question.

_____

S: I B / E: 4

Math Test Prep That Matters! Grades 3–4   Scholastic Teaching Resources

---

Name: _____ Date: _____

3 Dozen Roses

4 x ☐ = 36   36 ÷ 4 = ☐

1. Write about what you see above.

_____

_____

2. Ask a question about it.

_____

3. Answer your question.

_____

Number and Operations

Name: _____ Date: _____

$4 \times 5 =$ ▢

$40 \times 5 =$ ▢

$400 \times 50 =$ ▢

$4,000 \times 50 =$ ▢

$4,000 \times 500 =$ ▢

1. Write about what you see above.

_____

_____

2. Ask a question about it.

_____

_____

3. Answer your question.

_____

_____

S: I C / E: 1

Number and Operations

Name: _____ Date: _____

$56 \div 8 =$ ▢

$72 \div 9 =$ ◯

$8 \times$ ▢ $= 56$

$9 \times$ ◯ $= 72$

1. Write about what you see above.

_____

_____

2. Ask a question about it.

_____

_____

3. Answer your question.

_____

_____

S: I C / E: 1

Number and Operations

Name: _____ Date: _____

$.89

$1.30

1. Write about what you see above.

_____
_____

2. Ask a question about it.

_____
_____

3. Answer your question.

_____
_____

S: I C / E: 4

Math Test Prep That Matters! Grades 3–4   Scholastic Teaching Resources

---

Number and Operations

Name: _____ Date: _____

Money I Have:

Bills I Must Pay:

Gas	$80.00
Electricity	$90.00
Telephone	$40.00

1. Write about what you see above.

_____
_____

2. Ask a question about it.

_____
_____

3. Answer your question.

_____
_____

Name: _____   Date: _____

Bernice had a
birthday party.
Each of her five
friends ate one and
one-half mini pizzas.

Model/Picture

◯ —— $\times 1\frac{1}{2}$ = ☐

1. Write about what you see above.

_____
_____

2. Ask a question about it.

_____
_____

3. Answer your question.

_____
_____

S: I C / E: 4

Name: _____   Date: _____

Seating in the Auditorium

240 students

| A | B | C | D | E |

1. Write about what you see above.

_____
_____

2. Ask a question about it.

_____
_____

3. Answer your question.

_____
_____

S: I C / E: 2, 3

Name: _____   Date: _____

0.25   +   0.15

1. Write about what you see above.

_____

2. Ask a question about it.

_____

3. Answer your question.

_____

S: I C / E: 5

Name: _____   Date: _____

one whole   one whole   one whole

A   B   C

1. Write about what you see above.

_____

2. Ask a question about it.

_____

3. Answer your question.

_____

S: I C / E: 5

Name: _____ Date: _____

Number of Cubes	1	2	3	4
Total Surface Area	6 sq. cm.	10 sq. cm.	14 sq. cm.	

1. Write about what you see above.

_____

2. Ask a question about it.

_____

3. Answer your question.

_____

S: II A / E: 2

Name: _____ Date: _____

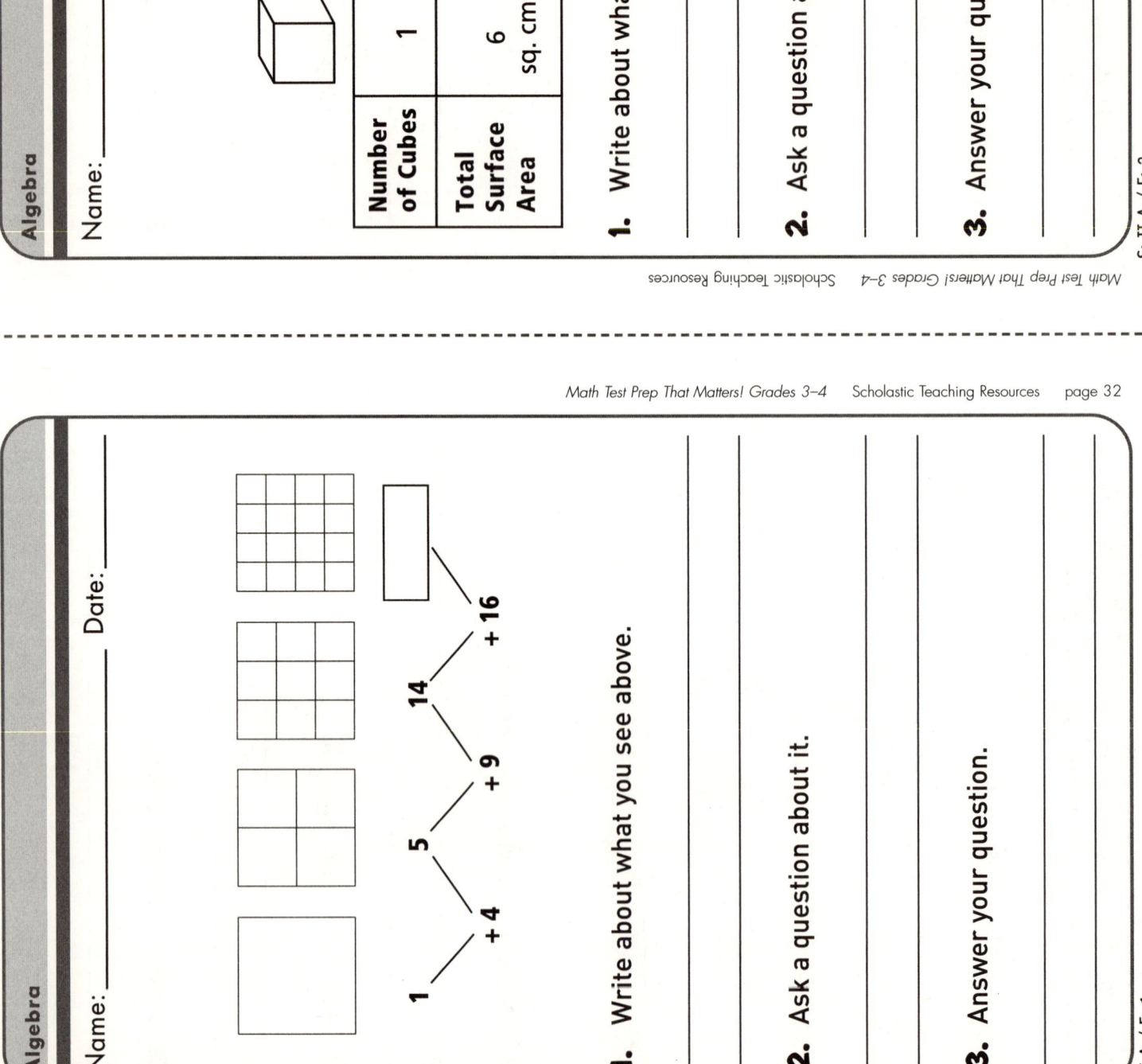

1   5   14

+ 4   + 9   + 16

1. Write about what you see above.

_____

2. Ask a question about it.

_____

3. Answer your question.

_____

S: II A / E: 1

Algebra

Name: _____ Date: _____

$P = 4s$

$P = 2l + 2w$
$A = l \times w$

w

l

1. Write about what you see above.

_____
_____

2. Ask a question about it.

_____
_____

3. Answer your question.

_____
_____

S: II B / E: 2

Algebra

Name: _____ Date: _____

THINK:
Commutative and
Distributive Properties
of Multiplication

A

B

C

1. Write about what you see above.

_____
_____

2. Ask a question about it.

_____
_____

3. Answer your question.

_____
_____

S: II B / E: 1

Name: _____ Date: _____

Today's Sandwich Special

#3.25

Number of Sandwiches	Cost
1	$3.25
	$6.50
3	
4	

1. Write about what you see above.

_____
_____

2. Ask a question about it.

_____
_____

3. Answer your question.

_____
_____

S: II C / E: 1

Name: _____ Date: _____

$$(4 \times 1) + 2 \qquad (4 \times 2) + 2 \qquad (4 \times 3) + 2$$

Surface Area = 4 x n + 2

1. Write about what you see above.

_____
_____

2. Ask a question about it.

_____
_____

3. Answer your question.

_____
_____

S: II B / E: 3

Name: _____ Date: _____

Temperature

Normal High	3/18	50 degrees
Normal Low	3/18	36 degrees
Temp. at Noon	3/18	34 degrees
Record High	1989	77 degrees
Record Low	1916	7 degrees

1. Write about what you see above.

_____

_____

2. Ask a question about it.

_____

3. Answer your question.

_____

S: II C / E: 1

Name: _____ Date: _____

Sunrise and Sunset Data

Date	Day	Sunrise	Sunset
3/19	Friday	5:59 A.M.	6:08 P.M.
3/20	Saturday	5:57 A.M.	6:09 P.M.
3/21	Sunday	5:55 A.M.	6:10 P.M.

1. Write about what you see above.

_____

_____

2. Ask a question about it.

_____

3. Answer your question.

_____

S: II C / E: 1

Name: _____ Date: _____

Draw any three triangles!

Acute
Equilateral
Isosceles
Right
Obtuse
Scalene

1. Write about what you see above.

_____

_____

2. Ask a question about it.

_____

_____

3. Answer your question.

_____

_____

S: III A / E: 1, 2

Math Test Prep That Matters! Grades 3–4   Scholastic Teaching Resources

---

Name: _____ Date: _____

A

B

C

D

1. Write about what you see above.

_____

_____

2. Ask a question about it.

_____

_____

3. Answer your question.

_____

_____

Geometry

Name: _____   Date: _____

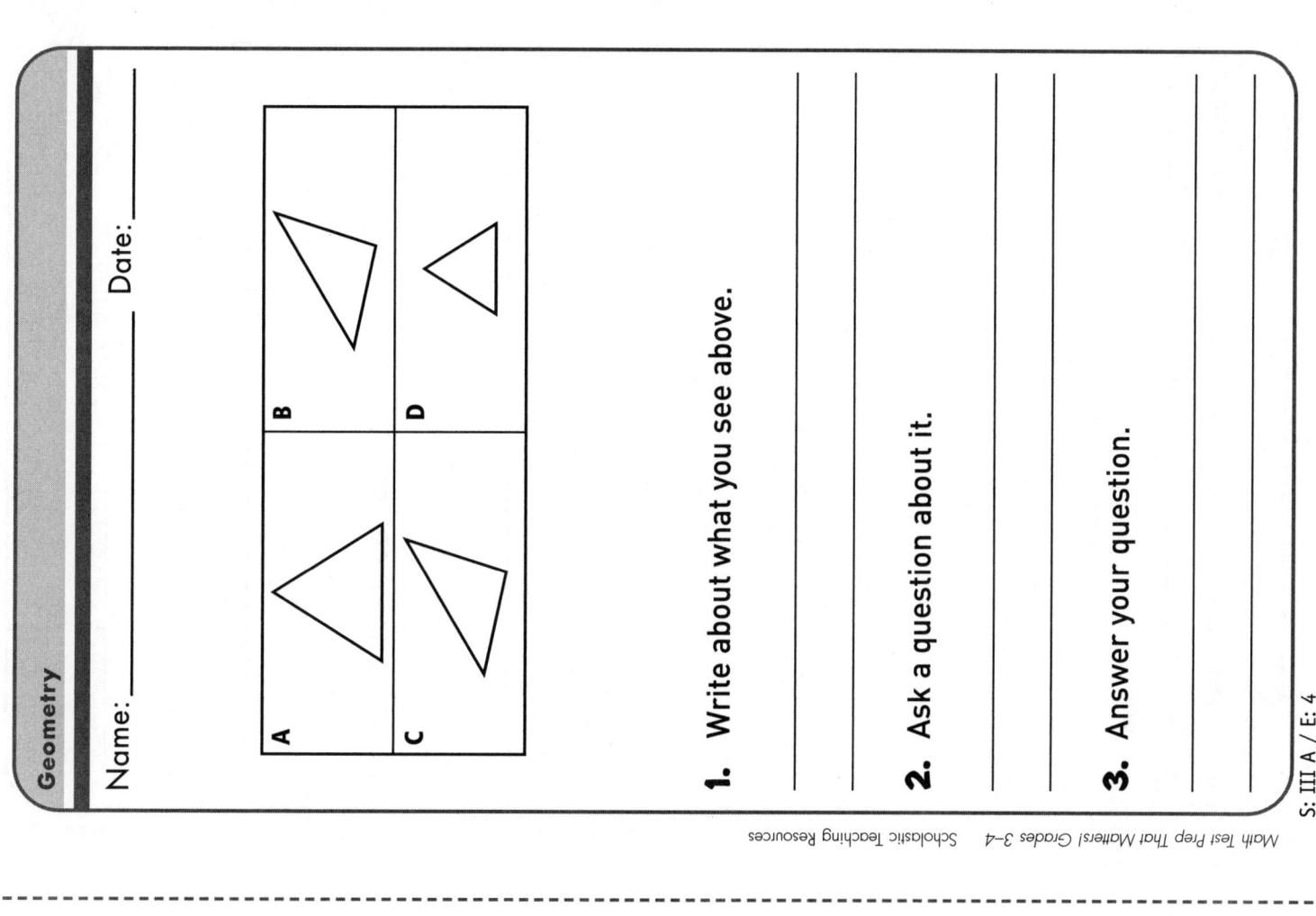

1. Write about what you see above.

_____

_____

2. Ask a question about it.

_____

_____

3. Answer your question.

_____

_____

S: III A / E: 3

Geometry

Name: _____   Date: _____

1. Write about what you see above.

_____

_____

2. Ask a question about it.

_____

_____

3. Answer your question.

_____

_____

S: III A / E: 4

Name: _____ Date: _____

1. Write about what you see above.

_____

_____

2. Ask a question about it.

_____

_____

3. Answer your question.

_____

_____

S: III B / E: 1

Name: _____ Date: _____

1. Write about what you see above.

_____

_____

2. Ask a question about it.

_____

_____

3. Answer your question.

_____

_____

S: III A / E: 5

Name: _____ Date: _____

How would you move from the point of origin to another point?

1. Write about what you see above.

_____

_____

2. Ask a question about it.

_____

_____

3. Answer your question.

_____

_____

Name: _____ Date: _____

A is at (1, 2)

B is at (3, 5)

1. Write about what you see above.

_____

_____

2. Ask a question about it.

_____

_____

3. Answer your question.

_____

_____

Geometry

Name: _____ Date: _____

1. Write about what you see above.

_____

2. Ask a question about it.

_____

3. Answer your question.

_____

S: III C / E: 1, 2

Geometry

Name: _____ Date: _____

A   B

F   ⌐|

C   D

⌐⌐   F

1. Write about what you see above.

_____

2. Ask a question about it.

_____

3. Answer your question.

_____

S: III C / E: 1

Name: _____ Date: _____

1. Write about what you see above.

_____

_____

2. Ask a question about it.

_____

_____

3. Answer your question.

_____

_____

S: III D / E: 3

Name: _____ Date: _____

A   **B**   **C**

1. Write about what you see above.

_____

_____

2. Ask a question about it.

_____

_____

3. Answer your question.

_____

_____

S: III C / E: 3

Name: _____

Date: _____

Shapes, Figures, and Lines at Home

1. Write about what you see above.

_____

_____

2. Ask a question about it.

_____

_____

3. Answer your question.

_____

_____

S: III D / E: 3

Name: _____

Date: _____

4   7   10

2.

1. Write about what you see above.

_____

_____

2. Ask a question about it.

_____

_____

3. Answer your question.

_____

_____

S: III D / E: 2

Name: _____ Date: _____

A   B   C

1. Write about what you see above.

_____

_____

2. Ask a question about it.

_____

_____

3. Answer your question.

_____

_____

S: III D / E: 4

Name: _____ Date: _____

1. Write about what you see above.

_____

_____

2. Ask a question about it.

_____

_____

3. Answer your question.

_____

_____

S: III D / E: 5

Name: _____ Date: _____

mm 10 20 30 40 50 60 70 80 90 100
cm 1 2 3 4 5 6 7 8 9 10

1. Write about what you see above.

_____

_____

2. Ask a question about it.

_____

_____

3. Answer your question.

_____

_____

S: IV A / E: 2

Name: _____ Date: _____

10 cm

10 cm

10 cm

1. Write about what you see above.

_____

_____

2. Ask a question about it.

_____

_____

3. Answer your question.

_____

_____

S: IV A / E: 1

Name: _____   Date: _____

Width of Students' Hand Spans (cm)

Name	Estimate	Actual	Difference
Ryan	18 cm	19 cm	1 cm
Keith	21 cm	21 cm	0
Maria	16 cm	18 cm	2 cm
Wilma	12 cm	14 cm	2 cm
Janet	15 cm	20 cm	5 cm

1. Write about what you see above.

_____

2. Ask a question about it.

_____

3. Answer your question.

_____

S: IV A / E: 4

Name: _____   Date: _____

Heights of Students

Name	cm	m
Franco	148	1.48
Pablo	139	1.39
Keisha		1.41
Kevin	145	

1. Write about what you see above.

_____

2. Ask a question about it.

_____

3. Answer your question.

_____

S: IV A / E: 3

Name: _____

Date: _____

Volume?

Area?

Perimeter?

1. Write about what you see above.

_____

2. Ask a question about it.

_____

3. Answer your question.

_____

S: IV B / E: 1

Name: _____

Date: _____

2 cm

8 cm

4 cm

4 cm

3 cm

3 cm

9 cm

1 cm

1. Write about what you see above.

_____

2. Ask a question about it.

_____

3. Answer your question.

_____

S: IV A / E: 5

Measurement

Name: _____   Date: _____

My Classroom

width

length

Name	Estimate	Actual	Difference
A			
B			
C			
D			

1. Write about what you see above.

_____

_____

2. Ask a question about it.

_____

3. Answer your question.

_____

_____

S: IV B / E: 3

Measurement

Name: _____   Date: _____

Measurement Tools

1. Write about what you see above.

_____

_____

2. Ask a question about it.

_____

3. Answer your question.

_____

_____

S: IV B / E: 2

Name: _____ Date: _____

one liter

one cubic
decimeter

holds
1000 ml

measures
10 cm × 10 cm × 10 cm

holds
1000 cubic cm

1. Write about what you see above.

_____

2. Ask a question about it.

_____

3. Answer your question.

_____

Name: _____ Date: _____

Area = 12 sq. ft.

Height = 3 ft

Base = 4 ft

Area = 12 sq. ft.

W = 3 ft

L = 4 ft

Area = _____

Height = 3 ft

Base = 4 ft

1. Write about what you see above.

_____

2. Ask a question about it.

_____

3. Answer your question.

_____

Name: _____ Date: _____

Favorite School Lunch Meals

Food	Tally Marks
Fish	HHT HHT HHT IIII
Burger	HHT HHT HHT HHT III
Pizza	HHT HHT HHT HHT
Taco	HHT HHT HHT I

1. Write about what you see above.

_____

_____

2. Ask a question about it.

_____

_____

3. Answer your question.

_____

_____

S: V A / E: 2

Math Test Prep That Matters! Grades 3–4   Scholastic Teaching Resources

---

Name: _____ Date: _____

Cans Collected

Amy	32	Ben	45	Carla	18
Dion	27	Edie	71	Franco	85
Gabe	68	Hector	56	Ismael	79

1. Write about what you see above.

_____

_____

2. Ask a question about it.

_____

_____

3. Answer your question.

_____

_____

Math Test Prep That Matters! Grades 3–4   Scholastic Teaching Resources   page 49

S: V A / E: 1

Name: _____   Date: _____

How Students Travel to School

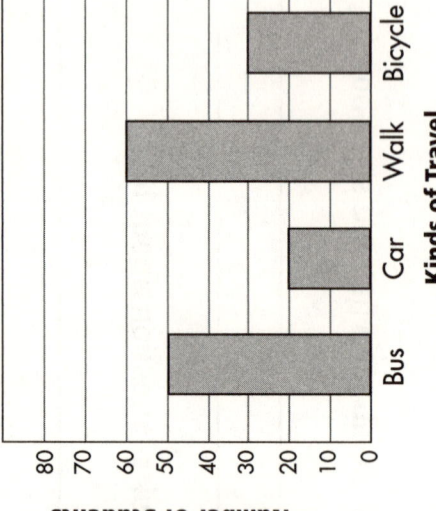

Number of Students

80
70
60
50
40
30
20
10
0

Bus   Car   Walk   Bicycle

Kinds of Travel

1. Write about what you see above.

_____

_____

2. Ask a question about it.

_____

_____

3. Answer your question.

_____

_____

S: V A / E: 3

Math Test Prep That Matters! Grades 3–4   Scholastic Teaching Resources

---

Name: _____   Date: _____

Our Investigation Of . . .

A. favorite lunch served at school

B. amount of time doing homework on Wednesday night

C. heights of students at three different grade levels in our school

D. _____

1. Write about what you see above.

_____

_____

2. Ask a question about it.

_____

_____

3. Answer your question.

_____

_____

Name: _____ Date: _____

Hours of Television We Watch

Hours of TV	Number of Students	
	Grade 2	Grade 5
No TV	2	5
Less than 3 hours	10	15
About 3 hours	15	12
More than 3 hours	5	3

1. Write about what you see above.

_____

_____

2. Ask a question about it.

_____

3. Answer your question.

_____

S: V C / E: 1

Name: _____ Date: _____

Books Read This Year

Number of Books	Number of Students	Number of Books	Number of Students
0	0	20	卌 卌 II
5	II	25	卌 卌 卌
12	卌	30	IIII
15	卌 IIII	35	II
18	卌 卌	45	I

```
      X
      X
X X   X X         X X
X X   X X   X X   X X
X X   X X   X X   X X        X
+--+--+--+--+--+--+--+--+--+--+--+
0  5  10 15 20 25 30 35 40 45 50
```

1. Write about what you see above.

_____

2. Ask a question about it.

_____

3. Answer your question.

_____

S: V B / E: 1-3

Name: _____   Date: _____

Reach In and Pick One Chip

Bag 1

Black chip	likely
White chip	possible
Black square	impossible

Bag 2

Black triangle	
Black square	
_____	triangle very likely

1. Write about what you see above.

_____

_____

2. Ask a question about it.

_____

_____

3. Answer your question.

_____

_____

Name: _____   Date: _____

What was the typical contribution? Hint: Think about mean, median, and mode.

Contributions to the Big Party

$2	$2	$4	$6	$6	$6	$10
$12	$12	$14	$14	$16	$16	$84

1. Write about what you see above.

_____

_____

2. Ask a question about it.

_____

_____

3. Answer your question.

_____

_____

Name: _____ Date: _____

?

0		0.5	0.75	1.0
impossible	less likely	equally likely	more likely	certain

1. Write about what you see above.

_____

_____

2. Ask a question about it.

_____

_____

3. Answer your question.

_____

_____

S: V D / E: 3

Name: _____ Date: _____

The Coin Toss Prediction

	10 flips	50 flips	100 flips
Heads			
Tails			

1. Write about what you see above.

_____

_____

2. Ask a question about it.

_____

_____

3. Answer your question.

_____

_____

S: V D / E: 2

Problem Solving

Name: _____   Date: _____

> For homework we have to use 16 pennies to form a square AND show a mathematical expression to explain it.

1. Write about what you see above.

_____

_____

2. Ask a question about it.

_____

3. Answer your question.

_____

S: VI A–D

Problem Solving

Name: _____   Date: _____

Problem

> At the end of the meeting, each parent shook hands once with the other parents, said, "Good night!" and left.

1. Write about what you see above.

_____

_____

2. Ask a question about it.

_____

3. Answer your question.

_____

S: VI A–D

Problem Solving

Name: _____   Date: _____

Place the numbers 1 to 9 on the grid so that they add up to 15 vertically, horizontally, and diagonally. NOTE: Use each digit only once!

1. Write about what you see above.

_____

2. Ask a question about it.

_____

3. Answer your question.

_____

S: VI A–D

Problem Solving

Name: _____   Date: _____

Each of the same shape in A, B, and C has the same value.

1. Write about what you see above.

_____

2. Ask a question about it.

_____

3. Answer your question.

_____

S: VI A–D

Name: _____ Date: _____

A 15	**B** 20
C 45	**D** 85

1. Write about what you see above.

_____

2. Ask a question about it.

_____

3. Answer your question.

_____

S: VII A–D

Name: _____ Date: _____

A (circle)	**B** (cube)
C (square)	**D** (sphere)

1. Write about what you see above.

_____

2. Ask a question about it.

_____

3. Answer your question.

_____

S: VII A–D

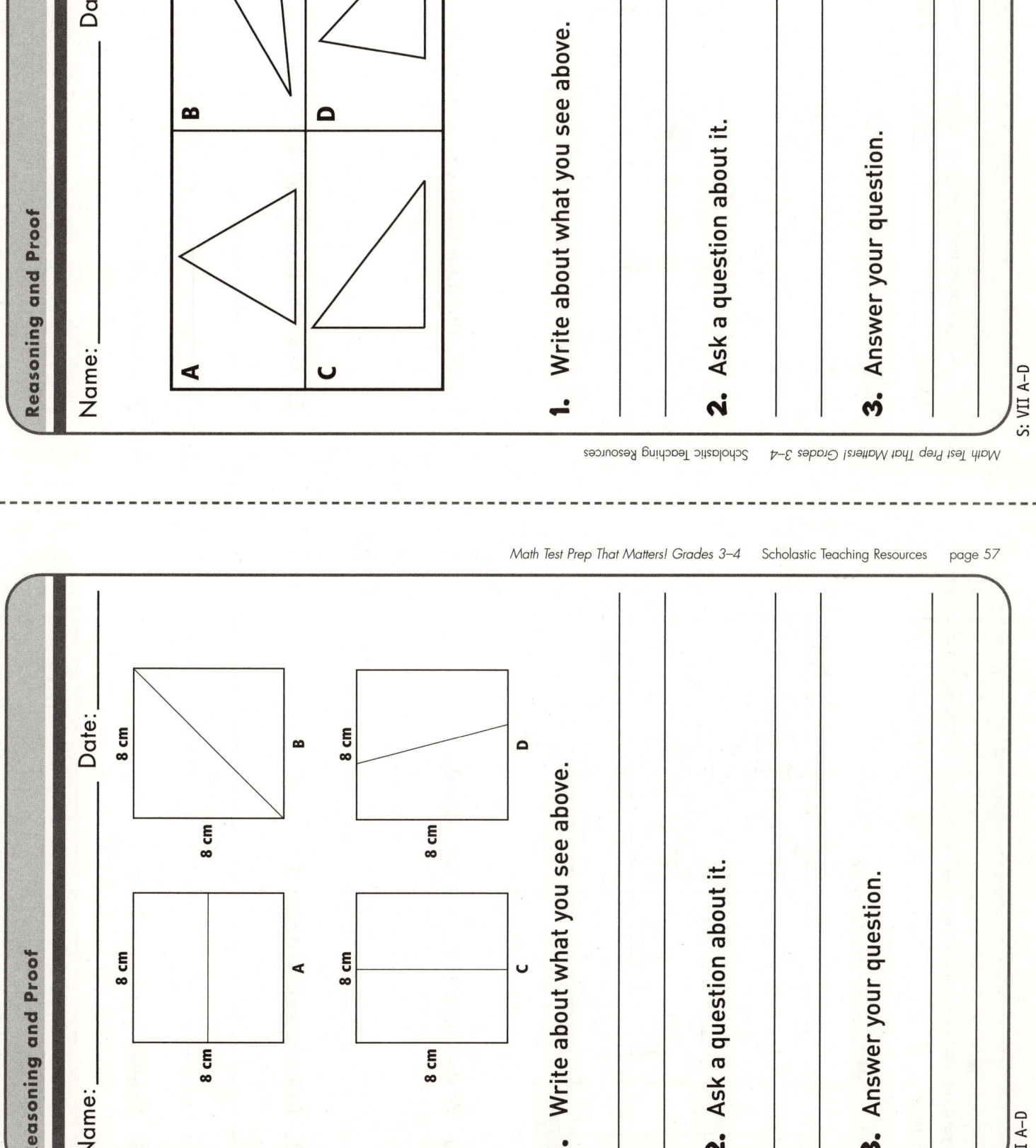

Name: _____ Date: _____

A   B
C   D

1. Write about what you see above.

_____
_____

2. Ask a question about it.

_____

3. Answer your question.

_____

S: VII A–D

Name: _____ Date: _____

8 cm   8 cm
8 cm   8 cm
A   B

8 cm   8 cm
8 cm   8 cm
C   D

1. Write about what you see above.

_____
_____

2. Ask a question about it.

_____

3. Answer your question.

_____

S: VII A–D

Name: _____ Date: _____

$$\frac{1}{2} \quad \bigcirc\!? \quad \frac{3}{8}$$

1. Write about what you see above.

_____

2. Ask a question about it.

_____

3. Answer your question.

_____

Math Test Prep That Matters! Grades 3–4   Scholastic Teaching Resources

S: VIII A–D

Name: _____ Date: _____

HINT: Each shape is an addend.

				Sum
▢	☆	◯	⬡	21
△	△	△	△	32
▢	△	△	☆	22
◯	⬡	◯	▢	26
Sum 24	26	28	23	

1. Write about what you see above.

_____

2. Ask a question about it.

_____

3. Answer your question.

_____

Math Test Prep That Matters! Grades 3–4   Scholastic Teaching Resources   page 58

S: VIII A–D

Communication

Name: _____   Date: _____

The Square Cake Bakery

The One-Pound Tangram Cake

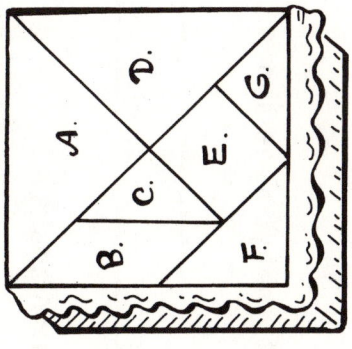

1. Write about what you see above.

2. Ask a question about it.

3. Answer your question.

S: VIII A–D

Communication

Name: _____   Date: _____

Place the decimal point in the correct place so that these numbers add up to 23.0.

$$24 + 32 + 105 + 63 + 6 =$$

1. Write about what you see above.

2. Ask a question about it.

3. Answer your question.

S: VIII A–D

Name: _____ Date: _____

A	B
	$\dfrac{3}{4}$
C	D
0.75	0.25

1. Write about what you see above.

_____

_____

2. Ask a question about it.

_____

_____

3. Answer your question.

_____

_____

Math Test Prep That Matters! Grades 3–4   Scholastic Teaching Resources

---

Name: _____ Date: _____

A	B
Q R S T	$A = l \times w$ $A = 4$ ft. $\times$ 9 ft. $A = 36$ sq. ft.
C	D
E F G H	18 sq. ft.

1. Write about what you see above.

_____

_____

2. Ask a question about it.

_____

_____

3. Answer your question.

_____

_____

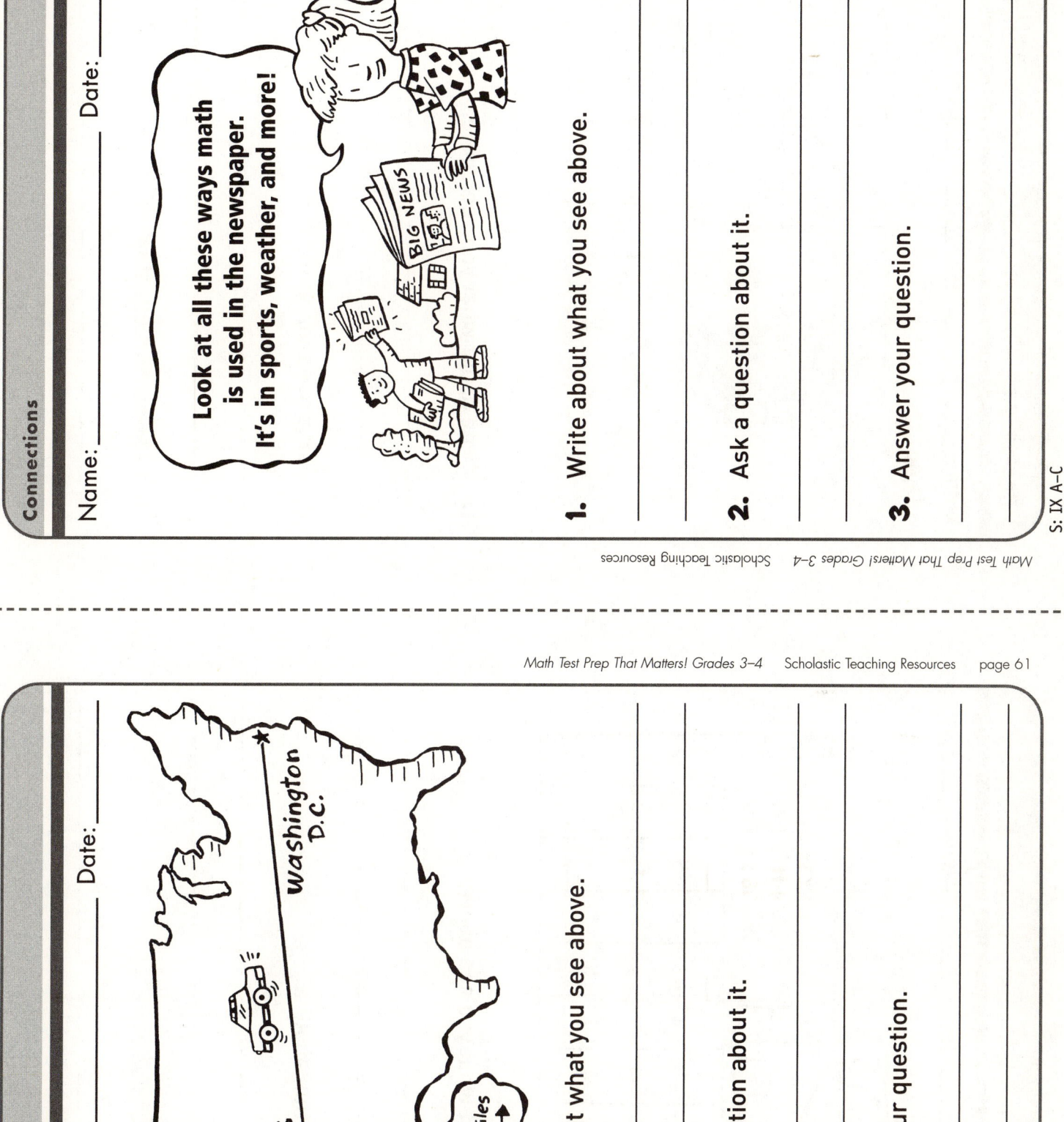

Connections

Name: _____   Date: _____

Look at all these ways math is used in the newspaper. It's in sports, weather, and more!

1. Write about what you see above.

2. Ask a question about it.

3. Answer your question.

S: IX A–C

Math Test Prep That Matters! Grades 3–4   Scholastic Teaching Resources

---

Connections

Name: _____   Date: _____

Washington D.C.

Los Angeles

1" = 662.5 miles

1. Write about what you see above.

2. Ask a question about it.

3. Answer your question.

S: IX A–C

Name: _____   Date: _____

$$\frac{1}{2} \times \frac{1}{4} =$$

1. Write about what you see above.

_____

2. Ask a question about it.

_____

3. Answer your question.

_____

S: X A–C

Math Test Prep That Matters! Grades 3–4   Scholastic Teaching Resources

---

Name: _____   Date: _____

Number of Squares	1	2	3	4	5	...	10
Number of Toothpicks	4	7	10			...	

1. Write about what you see above.

_____

2. Ask a question about it.

_____

3. Answer your question.

_____

Name: _____ Date: _____

Search for Patterns

x	0	1	2	3	4	5	6	7	8	9
0	0	0	0	0	0	0	0	0	0	0
1	0	1	2	3	4	5	6	7	8	9
2	0	2	4	6	8	10	12	14	16	18
3	0	3	6	9	12	15	18	21	24	27
4	0	4	8	12	16	20	24	28	32	36
5	0	5	10	15	20	25	30	35	40	45
6	0	6	12	18	24	30	36	42	48	54
7	0	7	14	21	28	35	42	49	56	63
8	0	8	16	24	32	40	48	56	64	72
9	0	9	18	27	36	45	54	63	72	81

1. Write about what you see above.

_____

2. Ask a question about it.

_____

3. Answer your question.

_____

Name: _____ Date: _____

$$243$$
$$\times\ 56$$

(□ × 243)

(50 × □)

1. Write about what you see above.

_____

2. Ask a question about it.

_____

3. Answer your question.

_____

Create Your Own

Name: _____   Date: _____

1. Write about what you see above.
   _____
   _____

2. Ask a question about it.
   _____

3. Answer your question.
   _____

Create Your Own

Name: _____   Date: _____

1. Write about what you see above.
   _____
   _____

2. Ask a question about it.
   _____

3. Answer your question.
   _____